"Evacuated"

"Evacuated"

By
Joan Davidson

First printed in July 2005

Reprinted December 2005

Published by
Design Innovations

www.design-innovations.co.uk

Written by Joan Davidson
and Suzette Savident

ISBN 0 95498 340 8

Dedication

I would like to dedicate this book to my sister Brenda, who has been my best friend all my life. And to my mum Florence Patch, who I loved with all my heart and miss very much.

Acknowledgments

I would like to thank my children, their partners and my grandchildren for all of their encouragement and support while I was writing this book, without them I would never have completed it.

Suzette Savident
for her encouragement to finish the book.

Mitch Bloomfield
Nicola Davidson
Patricia Carson
Heidi Savident

Audrey Mansell

Lawrence Ozanne
for all the help he gave me.

The Priaulx Library, Guernsey

The Bolton Evening News
for help with the pictures of evacuees.

Guernsey Evening Press

Foreword

On September 3rd 1939 Britain declared war on Germany. By mid June the enemy had swept through Europe and into France. The decision that had to be made by Channel Islanders was, whether or not to evacuate their children to the safety of the mainland.

This would probably be one of the hardest decisions that many parents would ever have to make. My mother was one of those parents who decided that sending her children to safety was the right thing to do.

This story is about my life as an evacuee.

Contents

1

"Leaving Home"

Guernsey, a small island in the Channel, South of England, just off France is my homeland.

I lived in one of four small cottages in a place called 'Collivets Yard' with my mum and sister Brenda. I never knew my dad; he died in 1936 a year after I was born. Across the road from where we lived was a coal merchant where my uncle, Mr Robins worked. Coal lorries would tip their load there and my uncle would bag up the coal to be sold. Brenda and I would spend time over there watching and getting rather black. I remember a rag and bone lady who used to call at our house, pushing a pram and chanting "any rags for Missy Martin". I was only five and would hide behind the door crying. Brenda would laugh at me and Mrs Martin would say, "Missy Martin won't hurt you", but this would make me cry even more. I can't remember much more about my life before we went away, except going to 'Trinity Sunday School' every week with Brenda, both of us would be dressed in our best blue velvet dresses and panama hats.

I hadn't long started school, when one day my mum came to meet me. The bell rang and I ran out as usual, except when I got outside I knew something was wrong. Instead of my mum standing there smiling as usual, she was looking upset. I asked her if she was all right, she just nodded and stood quietly watching for Brenda. Brenda came out of school slightly later than me as she was nine and she too noticed something was wrong. She looked at me puzzled, I just shrugged my shoulders. "What's wrong mum?" she asked. "Don't worry" mum replied, "I just need to speak to Auntie Dotty". We followed our mum to our auntie's house without asking any more questions. We would later learn that my mum had gone to my auntie for advice as she had to make the biggest decision of her life.

When we got home after visiting Auntie Dotty, mum told us to sit down because she needed to talk to us. She explained that the Germans were in France and there was a good chance that they would soon invade Guernsey. She said that most of the local children would be going to England, where they would be safe, and in the morning she would take us to school where we would be taken to the boat in a bus. We asked if she could come with us but she said that there wasn't enough room on the boat for all of the mums and dads, but it wouldn't be for very long and our teachers would look after us and when we came back she would be waiting. It must have been so hard to decide what to do, to keep your children with you knowing that it was almost a certainty that the Germans would invade the island, or send them away, not knowing where they would go or for how long. Looking back, Brenda and I both know that our mum did what she thought was best under the circumstances.

I will never forget that next morning. We walked to school carrying our bags, and mum started to cry while holding our hands tight. Once we had arrived at school we were given a square box with a strap, which contained a gas mask, we were shown how to use it, and told never to go anywhere without it. Then they put nametags on us; mine read JOAN PATCH. They started boarding the children on to the buses; they were crying and hanging on to their mums and dads. Parents were crying and hugging each other, as their children were driven away. Our mum hugged us both tight, and through her tears said "Don't be frightened girls; it is only for a short time, and then you will be home again", but we were frightened. I still didn't really understand why we had to leave and if it was dangerous to stay, what would happen to our mum?

As we climbed on to the bus, mum shouted "Look after Joan", "I promise" Brenda shouted back. We sat huddled together crying on the seat; at least we had each other. We watched our mum, crying and waving, as the bus pulled away, not knowing that it would be the last time we would see her for five years. The buses drove down to the White Rock Harbour, where a boat was waiting to take us to England. It was an awful crossing; the boat stank of fuel, and was really noisy, the sea was rough, and everyone was being sick and crying. I just wanted to go home.

When we eventually reached England we were put on to a train for our long journey up to Glasgow, and then at Glasgow we were put on to a bus and driven to a large hall. Inside there were mattresses and blankets all around the floor. We looked at each other both wondering if this was where we were going to live. Tired and hungry we sat down to soup and sandwiches given to us by the people who were there to meet us, but although the people were very nice, we were already home sick. After we had eaten I cuddled up next to Brenda on a mattress and was soon fast asleep.

Early the next morning we were woken, and given sandwiches and drinks for breakfast. Then all the children were sat down while a lady explained to us that there would be people coming to the hall to visit us all, but not to be afraid, as they were nice people who wanted to look after us while we were in Glasgow. It wasn't long before they started to arrive, and all day long one by one the children left with them. Each time someone came towards me and Brenda I would cling to her tightly, and the woman in charge of the hall would tell them that she would prefer us to stay together if possible because I was so young. It made us realise that some brothers and sisters were being separated. Eventually, a young couple arrived, and after some persuasion, agreed to take both of us even though they had only planned on taking one child. The couple told us their names were Mr and Mrs Adams, and that we would be staying with them. Brenda and I picked up our bags and gas masks and followed them to the door.

The Adams' owned a beautiful bungalow in Glasgow with a lovely garden, and a garage to the side, which we were soon to find out, was our play area for the whole of our stay. We were taken inside the house; I had never seen anything so perfect. Everything was spotlessly clean, and there was not a thing out of place. Mrs Adams showed us to our bedroom. It had thick carpets, frilly curtains and a really comfortable looking bed. I remember thinking that they must be very rich. They were both very nice to us, but you could tell that they had never had children of their own. During the day we would play in the garage, We had a little china tea set, which we would play with for hours, playing mothers and fathers with our imaginary friends. We never seemed to see any other children, and certainly never had anyone to play with, except each other. I expect we had other toys but the little tea set is the one thing that sticks in my memory.

When we went inside the house we had to be very careful not to make any mess and although Mr and Mrs Adams were good to us, it felt nothing at all like home. Brenda and I would eat whatever we were given for meals, as we didn't like to say if there was something we did not like. This was when I discovered how much I hated macaroni and cheese. I had never tried it before, but Mrs Adams seemed to serve it up quite often. Brenda didn't seem to mind, as she thought it was quite nice, but if I walked in the house and smelt it cooking, my stomach would turn and somehow I didn't feel hungry anymore, but would sit down and eat it anyway. Not that it was Mrs Adams fault as she had no way of knowing that I hated it, but I made myself a promise that when I got home I would never eat macaroni and cheese again, and I have kept that promise.

We had only been with Mr and Mrs Adams two or three nights when we were awakened by a really loud noise. Mrs Adams came into our bedroom and told us to put on our shoes, and a coat over our nightclothes. We quickly did as we were told, grabbed our gas masks, and followed her downstairs. We all hurried down to the end of the road where there was a huge common. A little way across the common was a tunnel which had been dug quite deep underground. Mr and Mrs Adams led us inside, it was cold, dark and damp and full of people, most of them were in their nightwear, with their coats over the top. The Adams realised how scared we were, and explained to us that the loud noise we had heard, was a siren to warn us that the German planes were flying our way, and that the tunnel we were in was a shelter to keep us safe until they were gone. We had to stay there until another siren let us know it was safe to leave. It seemed like we were in the shelter for ages, but it probably wasn't that long. I was so glad when the all-clear siren went, and we were able to go back home to bed. This, my first experience of an air raid, had been so frightening, and I hoped it would never happen again. But it was to happen many more times and became a matter of routine.

As time went on, I missed my mum more and more. I kept asking Brenda when we could go home, but she didn't know, and wanted to go home just as much as I did. Brenda started school but I never did, although I don't know why. I spent my days playing in the garage on my own, waiting for Brenda to come home from school and play with me. I never knew much about the Adams; they seemed to live very private lives. Mr Adams drove a double-decker bus, but that was about all I knew. We never met any of their family or friends, On the rare occasion Mr and Mrs Adams went out, we would stay with an old lady who lived across the road, I can't remember her name but she was very sweet. She would play board games with us and give us drinks and biscuits.

I am not sure how much time had passed, but I would guess about four or five months. It was a normal day; I had been playing in the garage as usual waiting for Brenda to come home from school, and was really excited when I saw her coming down the road. The days seemed so long and Brenda coming home was all that I had to look forward to, but as she reached the garden Mrs Adams called out for us both to go in to the house, I ran over to Brenda and hugged her and then hand in hand we walked inside. There was a lady sat in the lounge drinking tea, she smiled at us both but didn't say anything. We both smiled back and then looked at Mrs Adams wondering why we had been called in. she looked at us solemnly, and in a soft but determined voice told us that Brenda would be going to live with the lady, that she had only wanted one child to mind and she found that the two of us was too much. I couldn't believe what I was hearing; there must be some mistake, but there was no mistake, and within the hour Brenda was being walked out to the ladies car crying, "Please don't take her", I sobbed, I tried to run after her, but Mrs Adams held on to me. I don't think it is possible to put into words how I felt. I had been sent away from my mum, my home and my friends. Not knowing when, or if, I would ever see them again, and now they were taking away the only thing I had left, my sister, who I loved so much. Brenda was put into the back of the car, crying. I can only imagine how she must have felt, she too, had lost everything and was no longer able to keep her promise and look after me, the one, and only thing mum had asked of her. The car drove off, with Brenda looking back still crying, her hand outstretched against the window, as if trying to reach me. I dropped to my knees, staring at the car as it drove down the road and out of sight. A pain inside that would live with me forever.

After this happened, I would cry myself to sleep each night, praying that my mum or Brenda would come and fetch me, but I hadn't even heard from them, and was beginning to feel that I never would. Days turned to weeks, weeks turned to months. It had been so long and although I knew they would never forget me, just as I could never forget them, the war was keeping us all apart and I didn't know if it would ever end.

Then one day my prayers were answered. I was sitting in the garage playing with my tea set, as I had done so many times before, when Mrs Adams called me. I put down my little cup and saucer and ran inside, wondering if perhaps Mrs Adams had to go out and was going to leave me with the old lady across the road, as she sometimes did. I did hope so, as she had become my best and only friend, and I loved it when she had to mind me. But when I got inside Mrs Adams told me to sit down as she had something to tell me. Quite disappointed, I perched myself on the edge of a chair and listened while Mrs Adams explained that she had been contacted by the people who had sent me to live with her, and that apparently I had an Auntie, who had left Guernsey before Brenda or I was born, to live in Devon. She was called Ida, and she wanted Brenda and I to go and live with her. I sat motionless, trying to take in what Mrs Adams had said. She had said, Brenda and me, that would mean we would be together again. My heart was pounding, "Both of us?" I asked, making sure I hadn't heard wrong, "Yes" said Mrs Adams, and smiled at me, knowing that she had just given me the best news I could have asked for. She said that I would be picked up in the next few days, as there were things to sort out before I went. Although the next few days seemed long, they were quite bearable. I no longer cried myself to sleep. Instead, I would lie in bed thinking of Brenda, and us living together again. Maybe this was just the start and the war would soon be over, then we could go home. I at least again believed this would eventually happen.

When the day finally arrived for me to leave I had mixed emotions, I had lived with the Adams for nearly a year, and although they weren't exactly ideal parents I knew that they had cared for me the best they knew how, and even though I didn't love them I knew I would miss them.

Saying goodbye to the old lady across the road was the hardest. She was my best friend, and I knew she was as sad for me to go, as I was to say goodbye. But she hugged me and told me that she was pleased that I was going to live with my sister again, and asked me to give Brenda her love. Although leaving her was hard, the excitement of seeing Brenda again outweighed any emotions I had of leaving. By the time the car arrived to pick me up, I had been stood at the front door with my bag and gas mask for quite a while, waiting, wondering if Brenda was as excited as I was, and when I would see her. She might already be at our auntie's house, or like me, still be waiting to be picked up. But to my utter delight, Brenda was in the back of the car. Mr and Mrs Adams walked me to the car, gave me a hug and wished me luck. I waved to the old lady who was at her window, then jumped in next to Brenda. I hugged her as tight as I could, not wanting to ever let go. Brenda and I had no idea of what lay ahead. We were going to live with an auntie, whom we had never met, in a place we had never seen. But whatever was to come, we were together and that was all that mattered.

SS Viking - The vessel that evacuated the children to England.

Captain James Bridson.

(Top): 1st Officer Ned Gelling.
(Bottom Right): Captain James Bridson.
(Bottom Left): 2nd Officer Harry Kinley.

The evacuation of the schoolchildren of Guernsey
written by Captain Harry Kinley and read by Captain Peter Corrin

My name is Harry Kinley and in 1940, aged 30, I was second officer on board the SS Viking, an Isle of Man Steam Packet Company passenger ship which had been commissioned by the navy as a troopship. We were evacuating troops from the French Channel ports to Southampton, when we were ordered to proceed to Guernsey and to evacuate as many of the school children and their teachers as possible.

Navigating the waters around the Channel Islands was difficult but fortunately I had kept all the charts up to date and we had a very good ship's master, Captain James Bridson. We docked without trouble at number 1 berth in St Peter Port at 4 am. on June 21st.

By 9 am., the children were arriving in great numbers and I will never forget the sight of those thousands of children lined up on the pier with their gas mask cases over their shoulders and carrying small cases. From the age of four to seventeen they came aboard, many of them in tears. It was hard to keep back our own tears I can tell you. We stopped counting the children after 1,800 and with the teachers and helpers, there must have been well over 2,000 on board.

The ship was packed: every cabin, corner and space was filled. Going around talking to the children, I found that they had been waiting so long, that most of them had eaten the food their parents had packed for them. They were hungry poor mites. I went to Captain Bridson to report and he told me to strip the lifeboats of the provisions and distribute them among the children. Together with the crew, I went round with sweets, cake, biscuits and even condensed milk which we dished out in spoonfuls !

In my own cabin there were at least a dozen little ones with their Sunday School teacher. This lady gave me her prayer book and I gave her my Merchant Navy badge. Another lady gave her front door key to Ned Gelling our chief officer and asked him to lock her front door if the ship went back to Guernsey, because she had forgotten to do so !

We finally set sail at 11 am. Because we were a coal burning ship we were very conspicuous and a passing warship signalled a message " You are a pillar of smoke by day and a ball of fire by night and can be seen for twenty miles " we signalled back, " Thank you, we know." There were mines in the Channel and enemy aircraft overhead and we had one old gun and no escort. A plane did swoop down over us, which caused a bit of panic but it was one of ours which made the children cheer.
We said our prayers and zigzagged across to England with our precious cargo, eventually landing safely at Weymouth, where crowds on the quayside sent up a cheer.

As the children disembarked, I was standing with Captain Bridson at the gangway saying goodbye and I said to him "I wonder what will become of them all?" " So do I Harry " he said " I wish we could sail on to the the Isle of Man with them, they would be safe there"
From Weymouth, the children were put onto trains and taken, with their school teachers, to many parts of England and Scotland, where they were to remain for the next five years, as it turned out.

Many years later, my niece married a young man from Glasgow, who turned out to be one of those very same Guernsey children who had been evacuated on the Viking. He had not returned to Guernsey after the war but had come to live in the Isle of Man with the family he had been billeted with.

A Manxman myself, born and raised in a small island I could well imagine the feelings of those parents. Fearful of the German invasion and not knowng what lay ahead, they made that heartbreaking decision to send the children away for their own safety. I had many memorable experiences during the war years and a lifetime at sea but one I shall never forget is the evacuation of the schoolchildren of Guernsey.

Thanks be to God we made it

2

"Together Again"

It was a long drive to Devon, but Brenda and I had plenty to talk about. She told me all about the people she had been staying with, and what she had done during the time we had been separated. I was just so glad to be back with her that she could have talked for a week and I would have sat contentedly listening.

It was late in the day when we arrived at our auntie's. It was a house in the country, and as our car pulled up outside a woman opened the door. The lady who had driven us there climbed out of the car, and walked up the path. Brenda and I collected our things and followed. "I'm your auntie Ida," the lady in the doorway said, "You must be Brenda and Joan". We both nodded. Stood on the doorstep still holding our bags, we watched as auntie Ida walked the lady back to her car. They exchanged a few words and then auntie Ida returned to us and led us into the house. Inside was very dull and poor looking, what little furniture there was, was very old and there was hardly any floor covering. A complete contrast to the Adams house that I had just left. There were two young boys playing on the floor and a baby in a pram. Auntie Ida told us the boys were Stanley who was four and Henry who was two; the baby John was only a few months old. "I have another son," she explained, " his name is Roy, he is seventeen and was born in Guernsey". Just as Auntie Ida finished her sentence the door opened and a thick set man with very little hair stood in the doorway. He walked across the room and sat in an old armchair " This is Fred" said Ida " He lives with us and you are to call him Uncle Fred". Uncle Fred motioned for us to come towards him, Nervously Brenda and I edged forwards until we were stood a couple of feet away. Uncle Fred asked us our names and then said, "You'll be alright as long as you do as you're told".

Over the next few weeks we played with the children, and helped around the house. On Sunday mornings we would go with auntie Ida and get some Cider to have with our dinner. There was a place down the road where you could take a jug and they would fill it with cider for just a few pennies.

We hadn't been living there that long when one evening my auntie said we were moving house. That same night we picked up all that we could carry, the children were all piled into the pram and walked for miles with my uncle and Roy taking all they could in an old truck. Anything we couldn't manage was left behind.

They never told us why it had to be done so fast, and in the dark. We set up home again still in Devon but in another part of the county.

In those days there were plenty of houses to rent. We had even less furniture than before due to our speedy move, Brenda and I had a mattress on the floor right up in the corner of a bedroom, we had to put our coats over us at night to keep warm due to the shortage of blankets.

It seemed a very long time since we had left Guernsey. Brenda would ask Auntie Ida when we would be going home, but she would just say that the Germans were still in Guernsey and we couldn't go home until they were gone. We hadn't heard from our mum at all, but we later learned that she had sent Red Cross messages which we never received. Likewise she had not heard from us, we had no way of knowing how to contact her, and knew nothing about Red Cross messages.

Apart from the poor living conditions and the shortage of food, the worst part about living with Auntie Ida, was Uncle Fred. He was an angry, bad tempered man, who never seemed to go to work. We would lie on our mattress at night huddled together, listening to him shouting at our auntie. The children would be crying, but we were to scared too go and see if they were all right. During the day we stayed out of his way playing with the children in the garden.

Brenda and I started school, it was in a village a long walk from where we lived, but it was a nice walk with apple orchards along the way. Sometimes we would climb over the hedge and get the apples that had fallen from the trees. We knew we weren't allowed, and if we saw the farmer coming, we would hide until he had gone. Quite a few times we ended up hiding in the orchard most of the day, as the farmer had come to collect apples and we couldn't get back over the hedge until he was gone. This resulted in us being absent from school quite frequently and I remember one day my teacher giving me a candy bar for being at school for a whole week. Our school was quite nice and so was my teacher. We were the only evacuees there and I think everyone felt sorry for us as they all seemed extra kind. After school Brenda would meet me and we would walk home together past the apple orchards.

I don't know if on this particular day we took longer than usual to walk home, but when we got home Uncle Fred was waiting for us. We went inside to let Auntie Ida know that we were home, before going out in the garden to play with the boys. As we walked in the door we could hear Uncle Fred shouting at someone in the kitchen, he turned to face us, and shouted "you're late, where have you been?". We both just stood looking at him to scared too move, he was red faced and angry looking, and at the same time as he was shouting he was taking off his belt. Brenda and I hadn't realised that we were late, but even if we'd had an excuse, I don't think Uncle Fred would have wanted to hear it. Too terrified to speak or move, we both received my uncle's belt for the first time, but this would by no means be the last.

Sobbing uncontrollably we were sent straight to bed without any tea. We lay on our mattress crying, our legs red and stinging from the belting we had taken. I hated Uncle Fred and didn't want to ever see him again, I wished he would go away, or better still, we could go home. As the evening went on Brenda and I talked about what had happened. We both agreed that we would run home from school as quickly as we could from now on, and would never go in the orchards again, as we could only imagine what would happen to us if Uncle Fred found out about us taking apples, and missing school. We did as we had planned and as soon as the bell went after school, we would run home. But it didn't help, from then on every time something went wrong we got the blame, even if we hadn't done anything. Sometimes my auntie would know that it wasn't us to blame, but she would just walk away and let Fred belt us, and send us to bed with no tea. Although I don't think she liked to see him hit us, it was better he punish us than one of her boys, even if she knew it was one of them who had done what uncle Fred was mad about. Life became a living hell. We were scared to go home, but ran there as fast as we could after school because we were terrified to be late.

There was a little cottage we would pass on our way home from school, and very often the lady who lived there had talked to us as we walked past, only now we just shouted hello to her without daring to stop. But one day she called us over. "I remember you said how much you like reading" she said to Brenda handing her some hardback books, "you can have these if you like". Brenda was delighted, She took the books, thanked the lady, and we carried on running. All the way home Brenda kept saying how nice the books were, and that she couldn't wait to read them, and that she would have to keep them in our room so that the younger children didn't break them. I don't think that the lady had any idea how happy she had made my sister. Once we reached the house Brenda went straight into the kitchen to show my auntie what she had been given. Uncle Fred was sat at the kitchen table; he stood up, snatched the books out of Brenda's hands and threw them straight in the fire, saying that she didn't have time to sit and read, "There's plenty of work to do around here" he said "and if you think you've got time for stupid books you're obviously not doing enough". Brenda was so upset, her eyes filled with tears as she watched her books turning into ashes. We both already had a long list of chores to do each day, but Brenda's was now added to. Uncle Fred seemed to pick on Brenda, even more than he did on me. Although, he seemed to give me the belt as often as he could, he gave it to Brenda more. And although my legs didn't sting when he hit her, my heart would break each time to see her treated this way. The longer we lived with Uncle Fred and Auntie Ida the worse it got, and it seemed like we had lived with them a very long time.

One day Brenda and I had not long got home from

school, when a lady came to the door. I am not quite sure who she was but I think she was from the welfare. My auntie sent us upstairs while she spoke with the lady, so we don't know what was said, but when the lady had gone and we were allowed back downstairs, Auntie Ida looked worried.

It was a couple of days after the lady's visit that once again, late at night we collected together all we could and moved house. This time we set up home in Exeter, we lived in a flat above a corner shop right in the middle of the town. It was a lot smaller than the house that we had just left, but I somehow don't think Uncle Fred and Auntie Ida had moved by choice. It was here that I found out what air raids were all about.

The air raid siren was by a river, just a short distance from where we lived. And when it sounded it was so loud we would have to cover our ears, It was an awful wailing noise which we all dreaded to hear. Underneath the shop where we lived was a cellar which was where we had to go if the siren went off. We would grab the younger children, and all make our way down there as quick as we could, taking our gas masks with us. We never new how long we would be in the cellar, some air raids seemed to last a lot longer than others, and we could not leave until the all clear siren told us it was safe to do so.

Once the air raid was over we would go outside and there would be dust and rubble where houses and shops had once stood, there would be a smell of burnt wood and the dust would get in our eyes. People would be walking around dazed, and crying. The air raids Brenda and I had experienced with Mr and Mrs Adams, had been nothing like this, this was the real thing. We would hear the planes coming, then there would be a silence, then the terrible noise of the bomb flattening yet another row of houses, killing or maiming anyone in the area where it had landed. We would just pray that it wouldn't be us.

Brenda and I started school again, unfortunately not together. Brenda was now eleven, and too old to attend the same school as me. Auntie Ida took me the first day, I was really nervous, I hated starting a new school; I knew no one, and Brenda wasn't there. But after a few days it didn't seem so bad, not as nice as my last school, but I had made some friends and would rather be at school than at home with Uncle Fred. Although for the first time since I had met him Uncle Fred had a job. This meant that when we got home from school he wasn't there. I never played with my friends after school because although Uncle Fred was at work, I still had to go straight home.

One day when I got home, my auntie told me to take Stanley out into the garden and look after him. There was a small garden behind the shop which the shopkeeper used to let us use. I had this brilliant idea, I sneaked a pair of scissors from the kitchen and then led Stanley down stairs and into the garden, he had what I thought was very untidy hair with this big curl that sort of hung down his forehead, and I thought that Auntie Ida probably didn't have enough money to have it cut. So thinking how pleased Auntie Ida would be, I set to work. The first thing to go would have to be that big curl at the front. Stanley sat patiently, while I hacked away at his hair. What a surprise everyone would have when they saw it. When I had finished, I stood back to admire my work. It wasn't as easy as I thought it would be, but although it wasn't quite all the same length, I was pleased with it "Oh Stanley" I said you do look smart. Stanley felt his head and smiled, "thank you Joan" he said, lets go and show my mum. By the time we got upstairs Uncle Fred was home from work. Stanley and I, made our grand entrance, both as pleased as each other with my work of art. But instead of the look of delight I expected to see on their faces, there was a look of sheer horror. I looked at Brenda terrified, but I think that she was as shocked at what I had done as everyone else, and probably would have thought it was funny if she hadn't realised, just as I had, what I was in for. There was nothing she could do but stand there and watch. Off came uncle Fred's belt and I got the worst hiding from uncle Fred that I had ever had. But looking back now, that was the one hiding that I probably did deserve.

We lived in Exeter for quite some time, the air raids were frequent, and each one was as frightening as the last. Because I lived quite close to my school I would have to go home if the siren went off, as did any other children who lived close. I remember one day in particular, we were at school when the siren sounded, all the children who went home were running out of the school gate and I was running with them. I ran as fast as I could, panting for breath, the siren wailing in my ears. As I reached home, I could hear the planes overhead. I ran inside, and down into the cellar. Auntie Ida was already there with the boys. Air raids seemed worse during school time for two reasons, having to run home, and not knowing if Brenda was alright. This was no different than any other air raid, except the reason I remember this day in particular was the following morning when I went to school, I saw the road that I had ran down had been bombed, and the shops and houses that I had passed were flattened to the ground. I realised that if I had left school just a few minutes later, I would not have made it home

Months passed and everything stayed the same. Brenda and I would go to school, the air raids kept coming and Uncle Fred was as bad tempered as ever.

Then one night, we hadn't long gone to bed, when Auntie Ida called us. We got up and went to see what she wanted. Stood in the hall was a man dressed in a marines uniform, he looked ever so smart. Auntie Ida explained that he was my mum's cousin and that he had come to visit Brenda and I. He smiled at us and asked if we remembered him, but we didn't. He told us that our mum was fine, and that she had been trying to contact us, but hadn't been able to. So he had promised her that he would find out if we were alright and let her know but he obviously realised that we were far from alright, as a couple of weeks later without any notice, a lady turned up at the door. She told us to collect our things, as she was taking us to live with another family on a farm in Cheshire. We were sorry to leave the children, but couldn't get out of the door quick enough.

I never saw or heard of Uncle Fred or Auntie Ida again.

3

"Life on the Farm"

Once again we were on our way to a new home. It was a long journey to the farm in Cheshire, the weather was very cold and it was pouring with rain. We had been told that the people we would be staying with were called Mr and Mrs Jackson. We both sat in the back of the car huddled in a blanket, wondering what lie ahead.

It had been just over two years since we had left Guernsey, and I was finding it more and more difficult to remember my mum and my home, although Brenda remembered them clearly. I suppose it was because she was older when she left them. But I had lived in many places, and a lot had happened and Guernsey was just becoming one of them. The car pulled up outside a small farmhouse. As we got out, a lady opened the front door. "Quickly come inside in the warm," she said, and we all went in. There was a huge fire and Mrs Jackson ushered us over towards it. "Sit down here girls", she said, " You must be starving" Brenda and I politely informed her that we had eaten sandwiches on our journey, and weren't very hungry at all, just cold. Mrs Jackson looked quite puzzled; starving in Cheshire meant very cold. The lady who had brought us said goodbye then left. Mrs Jackson went out of the room, and then returned with two hot drinks. "Here you are" she said, "This will help warm you up". She seemed a very nice lady, I would guess in her late sixties. Brenda and I were sat by the fire, drinking our drinks, when the door opened. A man walked in and shut the door behind him. He had grey hair and a moustache and walked with a limp because he had a clubfoot. He smiled at us with the most kindly smile I had ever seen, his eyes seemed to twinkle. "This is Mr Jackson" Mrs Jackson said, we both said hello, "and this here is Brenda and Joan who have come to stay with us for a while". "Well girls" said Mr Jackson, "what do you think you should call us? You can't keep calling us Mr and Mrs Jackson all the time, how about Gran and Grandad". And so that was how it was. We all sat by the fire Brenda and I told Gran and Grandad a little bit about the places we had stayed, and they told us about the farm. A little later on in the evening a young man walked in. "Come and meet our girls Harry," said Gran "this is Brenda and Joan, they are going to be staying with us a for a while." Harry was the Jackson's youngest son he was twenty four and the only one they still had living at home, so Mrs Jackson must have had him quite late in life. Harry joined us by the fire and we all chatted for a little while longer. Then Gran realising how tired we were, showed us to our bedroom. For the first time since I had left Guernsey, I went to bed quite happy. I had a feeling I was going to really like it here.

It was quite late the next morning when we woke up. We had been so tired the night before we hadn't taken a lot of notice of the room which Gran had put us in. But now lying side by side in a large bed, we looked around at what was now our bedroom. It was quite a large room with nice furniture. Not posh like our bedroom at the Adams house, but cosy and sort of lived in. We could hear voices downstairs. "I think we had better get up" said Brenda. We both got dressed and went downstairs. We followed the voices into the kitchen. "Good morning you two, did you sleep well?" asked Gran. "Yes thank you", Brenda replied. I just nodded. I was busy watching grandad carrying a big metal container in through the kitchen door. "You're wondering what this is aren't you Joan?," he asked, and he smiled at me that friendly smile I remembered from the night before. "It's a milk can. I fill it up with milk from our cows, then I bring it to Gran, and she puts it through the cooler so that we can drink it". Gran told us both to sit at the table and she served us both a big breakfast with a glass of fresh milk. It was the nicest milk I had ever tasted. Grandad went back outside saying, in a joking sort of way, that he was too busy to stand chatting to us all day. When we had finished eating our breakfast Gran said "Get your coats on and I will show you around the farm".

It was only a small farm; there were six cows, some pigs, some ducks, a cockerel and some chickens. I thought to live on a farm with all these animals would be lovely, except for the chickens. I had been afraid of them ever since I was little. My mum had a brother called Stan; he was a lovely man who I loved very much and thought of almost like my dad, as I had never known my real dad. Every year he would bring Brenda and I a present on Christmas day, but was always playing practical jokes on us. One Christmas he gave us each a sack, we all laughed when Brenda all excited opened hers and found it was full of potatoes, but mine had a live chicken in it and when I opened it the chicken flew out at me, I was hysterical and it took my mum ages to calm me down, I was so frightened. My mum shouted at my uncle Stan saying it was a stupid thing to do, but he was so sorry and we knew he wouldn't have frightened me on purpose, so we forgave him. But from that day on I would not go anywhere near a chicken. Gran took us to see the chicken hutch first; it was a little wooden hut with small sliding doors at the back, so you could collect the eggs. Gran realised how scared I was of the chickens and told me to carry a stick to shoo them away. Which was what I did from that day on. Next we saw the pigsty, I liked the pigs, they were quite fat with little curly tails and they squealed when we went near them. Gran said it was because they thought we were going to feed them, and they would eat all day if you let them.

There was a huge barn full of hay and next door to that was the cowshed. We went inside and saw Grandad there, sat on a stool milking. "Have you brought me some helpers?" he asked. Gran asked if we wanted to stay and help Grandad, and we both said yes. "I have a very important job for you both", he said. There were loads of flies on the cows back, and Grandad told us that our job was to hold the cows tail while he milked her. "Otherwise the cow flicks her tail to get rid of the flies," he said "and it hits me across the head". Brenda and I both laughed, but took it in turn to hold the cows tail.

We both had a great day. Grandad showed us how to milk the cows; we fed the ducks and then explored the rest of the farm. In the evening Gran served up a lovely meal, she cooked in the hearth; there was a fire on one side of it, and an oven on the other. The food tasted extra good. I'm not sure if it was because of the oven, or just Gran's cooking, or perhaps both. But I know it was the nicest meal I had ever had. After we had eaten Harry came in. "Had a good day girls?", he asked. "Yes thank you" we replied. I am not quite sure where he worked, it wasn't on the farm, but I do know that he was in the home guards.

It was really nice living there. Gran did lots of cooking. She would make big fruit cakes, and her roast dinners were the best. Harry was really nice to us, he would tease us all the time, but in a nice way. We had our share of chores to do, like laying the table, helping with the dishes and helping Grandad on the farm with the milking, and the feeding of the animals, although only Brenda had to feed the chickens, as I was too scared. When all our chores were done we were allowed to play in the fields behind the farm. The fields didn't belong to

Gran and Grandad; they belonged to a farmer who lived down the road. But he didn't mind us playing in them. The fields were huge. Sometimes we would just play in them, but we also went in them to collect mushrooms. That was really good fun. We would stand in the middle of a field and look around until we saw a white dot. Then would race each other to see who could get to the mushroom first. Most days we would collect a small basket full, then take them home to Gran. One day when we were looking for mushrooms we found a nest where one of Gran's hens had laid some eggs. It was in the hedge, at the edge of the field, there where seven eggs all together, so we ran home to ask Gran if we should collect them. But Gran said that they wouldn't be any good.

There was always so much to do. Across the road from the farm was a large wood, where we would go to collect Pinecones and wood for the fire, and at certain times of the year there were Hazelnuts to pick. We would see rabbits darting through the trees and sometimes a squirrel running up a tree.

In the evenings after we had eaten we would clear the table and help Gran with the washing up. Then we would have our wash, put on our nightdresses and sit by the fire listening to the radio until it was time for bed. I remember our favourite program was a comedy, I can't remember what it was called, but it had Jimmy Jewel and Ben Warris in it, and Brenda and I used to laugh all the way through it. Our bedtime was 8 o'clock and as I was always tired by then, I didn't mind at all. But Brenda hated going to bed and would always ask me if I would like her to read me a story, I would say yes, but always fell asleep half way through.

We had been living at the farm a couple of weeks, when we were told that we would be starting school. The day before we started, Gran took us to buy some new clothes. We were excited as we hadn't had any new clothes since we had left Guernsey. I am not sure where Brenda's clothes had come from, but they certainly hadn't been anywhere near new and I had Brenda's cast offs. When we got home we put on our new clothes to show Grandad. "Well look at you two," he said, then turned to Gran and said "did you leave Brenda and Joan in town". We both laughed and ran upstairs. We got changed and neatly packed up our new clothes ready for the morning. That night I had trouble getting to sleep and was glad when Brenda offered to read to me. I loved school, but was always nervous the first day.

The next morning Brenda and I were up early, and dressed in our new clothes went down to breakfast; Gran walked us to school because it was our first day. It was quite a long walk, passed some farms, a garage and loads of fields. The school was small, much smaller than any of the other schools that we had been to. It only had two classrooms, Brenda was in one and I was in the other. Gran told us that we would stay at school for dinner and she would meet us when it was time to go home. At playtime we were all given a bottle of milk to drink and at dinnertime we were given a cooked meal.

The food arrived at school in large containers, and was served up by the teachers. The food was really quite nice, and after our main course we were given dessert. Brenda didn't like hers, so I ate two.

As promised, Gran met us from school. On the way home she stopped at the garage and bought a couple of newspapers, one was for her and grandad and the other was for Mr and Mrs Latham who lived on the farm next to ours. We then went to the Latham's house, to deliver their paper and Gran introduced us to Mrs Latham, explaining to us that it was Mr and Mrs Latham's fields that we played in. The Latham's farm was much bigger than the one we lived on; it had lots of cows and some horses. Mrs Latham seemed very nice, she had a little girl who was about three years old, called Jean, and while Gran and Mrs Latham had a chat I played with her. When it was time to leave, I asked Mrs Latham if I could come back and play with Jean another time and she said, that if it was alright with Gran, I could come over whenever I wanted.

After that first day at school we went on our own. Gran always had so much to do, and there wasn't much traffic where we lived. By the time we got half way to school we would meet other children and walk with them. We always had a bottle of milk at playtime, and a cooked lunch with a desert afterwards and very often Brenda wouldn't like her desert, so I would eat hers as well as mine. On the way home from school we would go to the garage and collect the news papers, then we would go to the Latham's farm to take theirs before we went home.

We had been going to the Latham's farm for about three days when for the first time we met Mr Latham, his two sons John and Marshal and their farm hand Alf. John was eighteen and Marshal was twenty, Brenda seemed to go all shy when she was introduced to them. We got to know all of the Latham's and Alf quite well, although I always tried to avoid Alf as he would tease me and sing. I would always dance with my dolly that had a hole in her stocking every time he saw me. Brenda and I both wore black stockings, but some how mine always ended up with holes in the heels, Gran would darn them for me but the holes seemed to keep coming back, and when Alf started singing I would get all embarrassed and blush, which he seemed to find quite amusing.

4

"Mums Letter"

It was a normal day, Brenda and I went to school and then on the way home collected the newspapers as usual. When we reached the Latham's farm I asked if I could stay and play with Jean, as I quite often did, but Mrs Latham said that Gran had asked her to send us straight home as she had a surprise for us. We were both wondering what the surprise was, and headed for home as quickly as we could. Running in through the gate we saw Gran stood in the doorway waiting for us. "I have a big surprise for you" she said and handed Brenda a letter. "It's a Red cross message from your mum" Brenda stood holding the letter just looking at it, as if she hadn't understood what Gran had said. Apart from our Mum's cousin telling us that she was alright, we had not heard from her since we had left home three years ago. "Are you going to read it," I asked, I don't think I quite realised just how Brenda was feeling. I had missed my mum for a very long time, but had gotten used to living with other people and no longer went to bed wishing I were home, I didn't even know where home was any more. Brenda slowly opened the letter and held it so that we could both read it. It said;

Dear Brenda and Joan

Hope you are alright, love you both, i'm fine,
See you soon, I know you're on a farm.

Take Care,

Love Mum.

Brenda looked up, tears streaming down her face. She obviously missed mum as much now as she had ever done. I hugged her not quite knowing what to say, I was just happy that we had had a letter and that our mum was alright. Gran smiled at us and said, "your mum was only allowed to write twenty-five words, but I am sure that now she knows where you are she will write again" Brenda dried her eyes and hugged Gran saying that this was the best surprise that she could ever have. "Well come inside and get your coats off girls" said Gran and you can write back to your mum and let her know how you are. We hadn't realised that we could write back to her and this brought a big smile to Brenda's face. Gran explained that we were allowed to write twenty-five words on the back of the Red Cross message, and that she would send it for us. We both sat at the kitchen table, trying to figure out the most important things to say in our letter, we wrote;

Dear Mum,

We are fine and happy to hear you are well, it is nice on the farm.

We both love you.

Brenda and Joan.

When we had finished, Gran promised to send our letter as soon as she could. After that first letter our mum would send us a Red Cross message whenever she was allowed, but that wasn't very often. At least we knew that she was alright, and she knew that we were being well looked after.

The nearest town to where we lived was Nantwich. It was about six miles away, and there was only a bus twice a week. Gran would catch a bus there once a week to do her shopping and she would also get shopping for Mrs Hedge. Mrs Hedge lived way up in the fields, in a small cottage with her husband, and daughter Joyce. Joyce would come to our house after school on shopping days to collect her Mums groceries, and Brenda would help her to carry them, as it was across lots of fields, over a turn style and across a couple of ditches, and there was usually too much for Joyce to manage on her own. Joyce was around the same age as Brenda and they became very good friends. Sometimes I would ask Gran if I could go with them and she would say that I could if Brenda and Joyce didn't mind. They would say that they didn't mind, but they would have preferred I hadn't asked, as it was the Latham's fields that we had to go through and I think both Brenda and Joyce had a crush on the Latham boys, John and Marshal. They would be looking out all the way up the fields to see if they could see them working, and if they saw them at the other end of the field, Brenda and Joyce would take a detour past them to say hello. The boys were a lot older than them and I think that they both found it rather amusing. I knew Brenda didn't really want me to go with her as I was so much younger than her and Joyce, but I would stick to Brenda like glue and follow her everywhere. At Joyce's house there were four geese, which would chase us every time we went there. I was really scared of them, and would run inside the house as fast as I could. Brenda and Joyce would laugh at me, saying they wouldn't hurt me, but I wasn't going to hang around to find out. Mr and Mrs Hedge were very nice, and Mrs Hedge would always give Brenda and I a drink before we headed back home.

I was so happy, I loved Gran and Grandad and our new home. We had friends to play with, I liked my new school and Harry was nice to us too. He would ask us to do little jobs for him, like run his bath, or fetch something for him, and he would give us sixpence for doing it. He was a good-looking man with dark hair and a lovely smile, and at the weekends when he went out he was always smartly dressed. I'm not sure where he used to go at weekends, as there was nowhere nearby, but I think it may have been somewhere in Nantwich.

Our school ran a bank, and as there was nowhere nearby for us to spend the money that Harry gave us, Gran suggested that Brenda and I opened an account to put the money in. We did as she suggested, and Gran started giving us sixpence each every monday to put in as well. We were given a card each and every time we paid in our money the teacher would mark it on our card.

At weekends we would do our chores in the morning, and when we were finished, would be allowed to go out and play. We would play in the woods, the fields, or sometimes just in the yard. We had made a den behind one of the sheds, and a table and chairs out of boxes, and Gran had given us some plastic cups and plates, we would collect blackberries, and sometimes would be given some biscuits for our tea parties that we would have. Some days Joyce would come and play with us, and if Mrs Latham was visiting Gran, Jean would be allowed to play as well, as long as we looked after her. She really loved the tea parties and would cry when it was time to go home.

We always found plenty of things to keep us amused, but if we did get fed up at all we would go and ask Grandad if he needed any help on the farm. Sometimes Grandad would take the cows to a field down the road to graze and we would help him. On the way to the field there were grass banks, and the cows would stop to eat, so Grandad would give them a tap with a stick and tell them to move on. Once Brenda and I had helped Grandad a few times, he told us that we could take them to the field on our own. This made us feel quite grown up to be trusted with Grandad's cows, I had never realised until I lived on the farm what gentle animals cows were, and was not at all scared of them. Brenda and I each found a stick and guided the cows out of the gate and down the road. Grandad had taught us to move the cows to one side of the road if a car came, but that wasn't very often, we got the cows safely to the field and once they were all in, closed the gate. We were so proud of ourselves, and ran all the way home to tell Grandad how well we had done. He said that from then on we could take the cows for him whenever we wanted to.

It had been autumn when we had arrived in Cheshire, and now a couple of months later winter was setting in fast. The weather was getting colder by the day, and the cows were no longer put out to graze. They were kept inside the cowshed, and fed on hay and bran. Brenda and I would help Grandad feed all the animals at the weekends because it was too cold to play outside for long. I hated the cold, and would sit by the fire in the afternoons listening to the radio.

Then the snow came, I had never seen such snow showers. Grandad would have to shovel away the snow to make pathways to the animals so he could feed them, and to the front gate so that we could get out to the road. It was very cold and would take us ages to walk to school and back. The snow was beautiful and we had great fun slipping and sliding on it, chasing each other with snowballs. When we got home from school we would make snowmen in the front garden, and very soon had a whole family of them. The snow lasted for a very long time and it was still snowing when Christmas arrived.

I don't think we had celebrated Christmas since we had left Guernsey and knowing it was Christmas Eve made no difference to us at all. We helped Gran to do the tea dishes and then after our wash listened to the radio until it was time for bed.

In the morning Grandad called us at breakfast time. We got up and dressed then went straight down to the kitchen but there was no one there. We could hear the radio playing Christmas carols, so we went through to the lounge and as we walked in, Grandad, Gran and Harry were all sat by a nice big fire. "Happy Christmas girls," said Gran, and gave us each a big hug, "I think these must be for you," she pointed to two piles of presents with our names on either side of the sideboard. Brenda and I were so excited; we each had a new jumper and skirt, two pairs of black stockings, two pairs of knickers, two vests and a liberty bodice and on the top of the pile was an apple, an orange and some sweets. We were absolutely thrilled; we gave Gran and Grandad a big hug and thanked them over and over again. We put our clothes up in our room and then came down to help Gran prepare the vegetables. Gran was cooking the big cockerel that had lived on the farm; he had always been really vicious, and had made Gran's arms black and blue on many occasions when she had gone to feed him. So we weren't sad that she was cooking him, and wouldn't mind eating him one bit. When all the vegetables were prepared we went and sat by the fire and listened to the radio with Grandad and Harry. We could smell the cockerel cooking and were starting to get quite hungry, we hadn't had any breakfast as Gran said it would spoil our dinner, so we were glad when Gran said it was time to lay the table. We sat down to eat, Grandad carved the cockerel at the table, and we had the most gorgeous Christmas dinner, with all the trimmings.

During the afternoon, there were all the normal chores to do, the dishes needed washing, the cows needed milking, all of the animals needed feeding and there were eggs to collect. We all did the chores together, and somehow it all seemed like fun rather than work. After our tea we all sat and listened to the radio for a while, then after thanking Gran and Grandad for such a wonderful day, we said good-night then went upstairs to bed.

Over the next few months we didn't go out and play so much. By the time we got home from school, had our tea and washed the dishes it would be starting to get dark. At weekends after our chores were done, I would sometimes go to the Latham's farm and play with Jean, and Brenda would go and play with Joyce. We always had to make sure that we left in time to get home before dark. It seemed to be a very long, wet winter but eventually spring arrived.

5

"In the Spring"

The farm seemed so different in spring. The grass was green, there were daffodils, buttercups and cowslips pushing out buds, and we could hear the birds singing. It made such a difference walking to school and back without the snow or hard driven rain.

We had just got home from school one day, when Grandad called out to us from the barn. "Come here girls," he shouted, we ran to him as fast as we could, wondering what was wrong. "Look what we've got here", he said. I just couldn't believe my eyes, one of the cows had had a baby calf, it was the sweetest thing that I had ever seen. It was trying to stand up and was wobbling all over the place. Grandad told us that we could help him to look after it if we wanted to, we said that we would love to and set about choosing a name for him. After much thought, we decided to call him Jack. In the evenings while Grandad was cleaning out the cow stalls, Brenda and I would clean out Jack's, he had his own sleeping compartment and we would take out all the dirty hay with pitchforks and put in nice fresh hay for him to sleep on. Then we would stay and pet him for a while, he would rub his head up against us and suck our fingers, we loved him very much.

Time seemed to pass very quickly. We seemed to have plenty to do from the time we got up, which was very early, until we went to bed. We had made friends with some of the children at our school and would walk home with them at the end of the day. One day on our way home from school, we were passed by a large convoy of army lorries carrying American soldiers. We were quite surprised when one of our friends shouted out "got any gum chum" and we were even more surprised when some of the soldiers threw out packets of sweets and biscuits.

The other children didn't live as far away from school as Brenda and I did so they only walked part of the way home with us. It was a couple of days after the convoy had passed when Brenda and I were walking home from school, we had done the first part of the journey with our friends as usual and were strolling along just the two of us, when we heard the roar of lorries coming down the road behind us, we both looked at each other, both having the same idea, "shout and ask for some gum" Brenda said, "you shout" I said. After a short debate we decided we would shout together, the convoy approached and red with embarrassment we shouted out a feeble "got any gum chum," the soldiers all smiled and waved and much to our delight threw out sweets, biscuits and chewing gum. We were so excited we picked up all the treats and ran home to show Gran and Grandad what we had. We did not get quite the reaction that we were expecting. Gran was absolutely furious with us, "don't you ever do that again" she said, "it's not nice to beg for food, and it's very dangerous". We hadn't thought of it as begging, the soldiers seemed happy to give us things, and the other children did it, but we saw how angry Gran was and told her that we wouldn't do it again, but we did. Every time a convoy passed we would shout and get rewarded, only we would make sure we ate it all before we got home.

It seemed all of the farmers and their families knew each other, even though their farms were quite aways apart, and we got to know them all too. Mrs Stewart who lived on one of the farms made cheese, and sometimes we'd go and watch her make it. She would mould the cheese into a perfect round shape or oblong block to sell, and it was fascinating to watch her. One day when we were visiting Mrs Stewart, Mr Stewart asked us if we would like to help him do the potato picking. We ran home and asked Gran if it would be alright, Gran said it was fine by her if we had the energy. By the end of the day we knew what she had meant. Picking potatoes was hard dirty work, but Mr Stewart told us to stop whenever we wanted to and Brenda and I had good fun while we were working. At the end of the day Mr Stewart let us ride on his old carthorse back to his house, Brenda thought it was great but I was a bit nervous. Mrs Stewart gave us both a drink of lemonade and some cheese to give to Gran before we left

After school when we had done our chores we very often spent our time looking for birds nests. We would only take one egg from a nest so that the bird would still have some eggs to hatch, and we would be very careful not to touch the eggs that we were leaving. Grandad had shown us how to make a small hole in both ends of the eggs without breaking them, we would empty the egg by blowing through one of the holes and then keep the empty shells in a box lined with soft paper, We had quite a collection. We had a skylarks egg, that we had found in some very long grass, there were quite a few ponds around so Brenda and I would lay planks of wood to walk across to the rushes and we would find water hens eggs and duck eggs. Then we would look in the bushes to see what other eggs we could find.

One of Gran's hens was nesting, so every day when we got home from school, we would run to see if the eggs had hatched, we were ever so excited when finally they did. There were six baby chicks and they were ever so sweet. We helped Grandad to make a run with some wire mesh across the top so that the crows couldn't get them. There where lots of crows in the woods across the road from the farm and we would very often see them fly off with a baby wild duck, or baby bird. Unfortunately, two of the baby chicks managed to escape from their run and before we could get there the crows flew off with them, I ran inside to Gran crying and Gran said that she would get Grandad to secure the run so that no more could get out, and luckily the other four survived

Before we knew it, it was haymaking time, and that was the best time of all. When it was time to cut Grandad's hay, Mr Latham came to help, along with a few of the other farmers. Mr Latham brought his horse and cart, and his tractor with blades on the back. While the blades cut through the grass, Brenda and I sat on the gate and watched. After a few minutes the rabbits started to dart out and run all over the field. We jumped down off the gate and tried to catch them, but of course they were much too fast. It took a long time to harvest a whole field as the fields were quite big, and during the day Gran arrived with a picnic basket full of drinks and sandwiches for all the workers and us. We all sat down on the cut grass to have a picnic, and then when we were finished, Brenda and I took the basket back down to Gran. Eventually all of the hay was cut and we helped to collect it up to put into bails. The men loaded the bails onto the cart and Grandad let us sit right on the top of the hay to ride home. That evening we were so tired that even Brenda didn't mind going to bed. We said good night to Gran and asked her if we could help Grandad again in the morning, Gran said it would be alright as long as we didn't get in the way, as it was Mr Latham's hay that they would be cutting.

We had started our summer holidays now, and Gran said that if we wanted to we could go to Nantwich with her on shopping day. "Why don't you pick some mushrooms" Grandad said "you could sell them to the market," so that's what we did. On shopping day we set off to catch the bus with two big baskets of mushrooms that we had collected the day before. We had to leave home quite early, as it was a long way to Nantwich, which was probably why Gran didn't take us very often.

When we arrived in Nantwich Gran took us straight to the market with our mushrooms, we didn't have any trouble at all selling them. The lady running the market stall paid us and after sharing the money, we set out to find something to buy. I bought a bracelet with my share, and Brenda finally, after checking out every stall, decided on some ribbons and slides for her hair. Gran did her shopping, and then she took us to visit two ladies that were related to her and Grandad. They lived only a few minutes walk from the shopping centre. They seemed really pleased to see Gran and invited us in. They made us all a drink and then asked us to tell them about where we had come from, and the places that we had stayed. They made us very welcome and it was obvious they really liked Gran. After a while Gran said it was time to go for the bus, both of the ladies gave us all a hug and made us promise to visit again soon. When we got home we went straight to show Grandad what we had bought, and we caught Harry as he came in from work to show him as well, we were both really pleased with what we had chosen, and asked Gran if we could collect and sell mushrooms again, next time she went to town, Harry laughed and said that Gran had better watch out or we would be asking for our own market stall before long. Joyce arrived for her mum's shopping and Brenda helped her to carry it, this was one time that Brenda didn't have me tagging along as I was too tired to go all the way up the fields. It had been a long day, but a good one.

One Sunday when we went in for tea there was a young woman sat at the table next to Harry. "Here they are now," Harry said as we walked in "this is Brenda and Joan, my favourite girls that I told you about, and this is Betty" Harry said motioning towards the woman. We said hello, "I have heard a lot about you both" Betty said. We had tea then Gran and Grandad sat chatting with Harry and Betty while Brenda and I washed the dishes, then Harry said he was going to take Betty home, we all said goodbye, Betty thanked Gran for tea and said that she hoped that she would see us again soon then left with Harry. Betty visited occasionally for tea after that and I realised that she was Harry's girlfriend, but she lived in Nantwich so it wasn't very often that she came. Harry spoke about her all the time so I knew that they were still together and that he liked her a lot.

One of the highlights of the summer was the Gymkhanas; these were shows that would be held in a field. Some of the women would make cakes and sandwiches, the horses would all be dressed up in there finest harnesses and ribbons. There was horse racing and show jumping with silver cups to be won, and games for the children. There were stalls that sold cakes, sweets, toffee apples, drinks and lots of home produce.

Brenda, Joyce and I would join in all the games. At the end of the day everyone would sit at long tables and have a picnic tea. There would be three or four Gymkhanas throughout the summer at different farms and we went to all of them, they were really great days out.

One of the good things about living in Cheshire, was there was never any air raids. The Germans only ever seemed to bomb the cities, airports and harbours. Apart from the rationing of food we wouldn't have even known that there was a war on. Except, one day we were playing out in the yard when we heard a plane fly overhead, we both looked up and saw that it was very low and still heading downwards. Just as the plane got out of sight we heard an almighty crash. The plane had crashed in a field not far away. Gran and Grandad started running in the direction of the plane to see if there was anything that they could do to help, Brenda and I following close behind. But by the time we got there, quite a few of the other farmers were already there. They said that the plane wasn't safe to go by and that we all had to keep our distance until the police and ambulance arrived. The plane had nosed dived into the field, and the wreckage was spread everywhere. Gran said we were best to go home if there was nothing we could do to help. Brenda and I wanted to stay and watch, but did as we were told and followed Gran and Grandad back home. We later learned that it had been a German plane and that the pilot had been killed outright. This incident reminded us that although it was peaceful in Cheshire, most of the country were still experiencing terrible and frightening times, just as we had in Exeter.

Brenda and I had been invited to a birthday party. It was a girl from our school called Elizabeth that had invited us and we were very excited. We never went to parties so it was quite a special occasion for us. Gran had bought us a present to take, dressed up in our best clothes we set off to Elizabeth's house.

When we first arrived, I just sat watching the others play as I was to shy to join in, but there were quite a few children from our school there and it didn't take long before I was playing as well. After we had played a few games we had tea, there were sandwiches and sausage rolls and for afters Elizabeth's mum had made jelly in cake papers with whipped cream on top. As I went to eat my jelly the cake paper ripped, and the jelly and cream spilt all over the tablecloth, I was so embarrassed but nobody seemed to mind. When we had all finished eating, Elizabeth's mum brought in a birthday cake with candles, and we all sang happy birthday. Then we played more games, I was fine and having a great time until they played a game called postman's knock. The idea of the game was that someone would leave the room, and while they waited outside, everyone else was given a number. The person who had been waiting outside would be called back in and they would have to shout a number out. If the number was yours you had to kiss them. I thought this was great fun and laughed when Brenda's number was shouted and she had to kiss Tommy who was in my class, but a few turns later a little boy called out my number, I didn't want to kiss him but I didn't know what to do, then all of a sudden I started to cry. The other children not quite knowing what to do with me said that if I wanted I could sing a song instead, so that was what I did. When the party was over, Elizabeth's mum gave everyone a piece of birthday cake to take home. Brenda and I put on our coats and thanked Elizabeth for inviting us, then started walking home. It was quite a walk, Elizabeth's house was about half way between our house and school and it was starting to get dark. When we got about half way home we saw Gran walking towards us, "where have you been" she said in a cross voice, "you should have left the party before it started getting dark, I was worried" we told her that we were sorry but we had not realised how late it was and that the party had just finished. Gran said that she forgave us but never to be late again.

On the way home we told Gran all about the party and Brenda told her about me crying, " it was so embarrassing" Brenda said, Gran put her arm around my shoulder and said, "Never mind Joan, I am sure that when you are older you'll enjoy playing postman's knock". I did love Gran, even though she shouted sometimes, I knew that her and Grandad loved us very much.

6

"Sad Times"

All too soon the summer was at an end and autumn was setting in. The weather was getting colder and once again it was getting dark early. During the evenings we would all sit around a big fire listening to the wireless and talking about the things that we had done during the summer months such as haymaking, potato picking and bird nesting and about the fun that we'd had at the gymkhanas. As we reached winter the snow started to fall. This was our second winter on the farm living with Grandad, Gran and Harry. We were still getting Red Cross letters from our mum but she wasn't allowed to write very often and you can't say an awful lot when you are only allowed to write twenty-five words. We looked forward to hearing from her and would always write straight back to her on the back of her letter. The snow got heavier, and once again needed shovelling away to make paths to the road and the animals. We started making another family of snowmen in the front garden.

It was not long before Christmas when one day after school Joyce came to collect her mum's shopping. As usual Brenda went to help her carry it, and as usual I insisted on tagging along. "I really think you should stay home," said Brenda, but I made such a fuss that in the end they took me with them. The snow was deep and by the time we got half way up the first field I was lagging behind, moaning because my legs ached from trying to walk in the deep snow. By the time we had got to the gate that led into the second field, both Brenda and Joyce had had enough of me. There was a cow trough next to the gate and the water in it had frozen solid, Joyce and Brenda lifted me up and sat me in the trough, "just stay there" said Brenda "I will collect you on the way back", glad not to have to walk any further I did as I was told. Brenda was gone quite a while, I sat there cold but quite happy in the trough, at least I didn't have to walk all the way to Joyce's house. Brenda and Joyce had probably gone looking for the Latham boys as usual but they should have guessed that they wouldn't be working the fields in snow this deep. Eventually Brenda collected me as promised, she helped me out of the trough and we both made our way down the field and home to a nice warm fire.

It was Christmas again, and again we had presents from Gran and Grandad. A pile each either side of the sideboard of clothes, fruit and sweets. For Christmas dinner we had turkey followed by Christmas pudding and custard. During the afternoon, after seeing to the animals, we all sat listening to the wireless. Gran had invited Harry's girlfriend Betty for tea so we helped Gran to lay the table.

Betty arrived and after Brenda and I had shown her the presents that we had received we all sat down to eat. After tea we helped Gran clear up while Harry took Betty home, then sat and listened to the wireless until it was time for bed.

The winter was cold and wet and seemed to last forever but eventually winter did come to an end. The trees again had leaves and the flowers were starting to bud. There was an air of excitement at the farm, although we didn't know why, but by the bits of conversation that we had managed to overhear and piece together, it seemed Harry and Betty were to be married, and quite soon. Brenda and I were both quite excited at the thought of a wedding but didn't let on that we knew anything as we were not yet supposed to know.

Then one day when we came home from school, Gran met us at the door. "You'll have to be quiet girls" she said, "Harry's in bed, I think he's got flu". Harry had come home from work early with a bad headache and feeling ill, we knew he must feel bad because Harry was never off work sick. We kept very quiet until it was time for bed. We had been asleep a few hours when we were woke by a noise coming from Harry's bedroom, we both sat up and listened, Gran was telling Harry to lie down and Grandad was telling him to calm down, they both sounded very upset. We could hear Harry shouting and moaning, "what's going on", I asked Brenda, but at that moment Gran rushed into our bedroom. "Quick girls get dressed, Harry's sick" she said, "we need to get help," Brenda and I got dressed as fast as we could and followed Gran downstairs. Gran grabbed our coats and a torch and the three of us headed off outside and down the road. It must have been about three o'clock in the morning, it was pitch black and quite cold, Gran was very upset and we realised that it must be quite serious. Grandad had told Gran to take us with her, as he didn't want her going for help on her own. We reached the Latham's farm and Gran started banging on the door and shouting out for help. Mr Latham answered the door in his dressing gown, "what on earth is the matter" he asked, Gran started crying, she quickly explained that Harry was going mad with the pain in his head, and that he was trying to get to the window. Mrs Latham had by now also come to the door. Gran asked if Mr Latham and his sons could quickly go and help Grandad to hold Harry down. Mr Latham wasted no time, he shouted for the boys, grabbed a pair of trousers and a torch and ran off up the road.

Gran asked Mrs Latham to call an ambulance as we didn't have a phone, then the three of us set off up through the fields to Mr and Mrs Hedges farm to get more help. It was very dark and scary, we only had one torch and had an awful job to see where we were going, when we reached the style I fell over it and landed in the ditch on the other side. By the time we reached Mr and Mrs Hedges farm my feet were slopping in my shoes and we were all really cold. Gran frantically banged on the door until Mr Hedge answered, then after quickly telling him about Harry we headed back home. Mr Hedge had got dressed as fast as he could and by the time we had got half way down the first field he ran past us heading for our farm. We got home just before the ambulance arrived, the ambulance men went upstairs and a few minutes later came down with Harry strapped to a stretcher, they loaded him into the ambulance then with lights flashing drove off down the road. Grandad was very upset and Gran was crying, they thanked everyone for their help and the Latham's and Mr Hedge went home. Brenda and I didn't quite know what to say or do to make Gran and Grandad feel better, we both loved Harry and were quite upset, but felt sure that now the ambulance had taken him to hospital he would be alright. So feeling that we should maybe leave Gran and Grandad alone, we went upstairs got undressed and went to bed.

The following morning we went to school as usual. Gran had been very quiet at breakfast, we knew it was because she was worried about Harry, but at least he was now in hospital and in good hands. After school we collected the newspapers from the garage and delivered the Latham's as normal. Then set off home wondering if Harry would be back from hospital, or if Gran had heard how he was doing. But we knew as soon as we walked in that the news was not good. Gran was sat in the armchair with Grandad hugging her, both of them crying. There were some people at our house that we had never seen before, Brenda and I just stood looking at everyone waiting for someone to say something. A woman came over to us and guided us into the kitchen, "you must be Brenda and Joan," she said, I was starting to get annoyed. Who were all these people and what had they done to Gran and Grandad to make them so upset. "I am afraid I have something sad to tell you," said the woman "Harry has died in hospital, He had meningitis and the doctors couldn't save him." I pushed passed the woman, ran upstairs and threw myself on the bed, sobbing, Brenda came in and sat on the bed next to me, I sat up and hugged her and we both just cried.

The days that followed were hard, Gran cried all the time, it was as though she had just given up. Grandad tried to comfort her but was hurting just as much as she was. It was awful so see them both so upset and the thought of never seeing Harry again was unreal. We couldn't imagine what it would be like to not have him teasing us or to hear him laugh, or see that happy smiling face that we had grown to love so much. The day before Harry's funeral Brenda decided that we should use the money that Gran had given us to put in the bank to buy some flowers. On the way home from school we went to the Darlington's farm, it was the next farm down the road from the Latham's. Mrs Darlington had a beautiful garden full of flowers at the front of her house and at that time the flowers were just starting to open their buds. We knocked on the door and Mrs Darlington answered, Brenda and I explained to her that we wanted to buy some flowers for Harry's funeral and that we had sixpence each to pay for them, and we wondered if she wouldn't mind selling us some from her garden. Mrs Darlington gave us a big smile, "you keep your money and help yourself to whatever flowers you want," she said, then she went inside leaving us in the garden. Brenda and I both started picking, we picked a few flowers and then a few more, and a few more until by the time we left Mrs Darlington didn't have a flower left in her garden and Brenda and I had a huge armful each. It was just that the flowers were so beautiful and each time we felt we probably had enough we would see some that seemed extra nice and we would just have to pick them. Poor Mrs Darlington must have had an awful shock when she eventually came out of her door and saw her garden.

Every day since Harry had died one of Gran or Grandad's relatives had visited the farm to help them, I think that they had worked it between them that Gran and Grandad would not be left on there own. It seemed as one would leave, another would just happen to turn up and offer to help with the farm, or cook tea and if there was nothing for them to do they would sit and talk to Gran and Grandad, not that Gran was talking much. We gave the flowers that we had picked to one of the visiting relatives and asked if she could put them on Harry's grave for us after the funeral, the woman said that the flowers were lovely and that she would be pleased to take them for us. I should imagine that they didn't all reach Harry's grave, as the woman would have had a job to carry them all, but as long as some of them got there, that was all that mattered.

The night before the funeral, Harry was brought home in his coffin. It was traditional that they spend their last night at home. He was taken straight upstairs and put in his bedroom. That night Brenda and I didn't get much sleep, we could hear Gran in Harry's room crying and it made us so sad, but there was nothing we could do or say to help her. The following morning we didn't have to go to school. People started arriving at the house, there were relatives, friends and neighbours, some we new, and some that we had never seen before. They had all come to see Harry and pay their last respects. Then the Hearse arrived to collect Harry, some of the men went upstairs and carried the coffin down and out of the door. Gran started crying uncontrollably and trying to get to Harry, "please don't take him," she was shouting, desperately trying to get to the coffin, poor Grandad was holding on to her sobbing, and trying to comfort her. By now Brenda and I were sobbing as well, in fact I don't think there was a person there who wasn't crying, the coffin was loaded and the Hearse pulled away. Gran and Grandad didn't go to the funeral, neither of them were in a fit state, in fact a couple of people stayed behind to look after them while the rest of the family and friends went to say their last farewell to Harry.

The next couple of weeks were very hard, talking to Gran and Grandad was difficult, we never knew what to say. They were trying very hard to get back to normal, probably for our sake as much as anything, but it wasn't easy. It was as though a big black cloud hung over the house, and there was great sadness in their eyes and voices. It was two weeks since the funeral and Grandad said he felt it was time that we all went and take some flowers to Harry's grave, none of us had been yet, Gran and Grandad had been too upset to go anywhere. We went to the church in Nantwich where the funeral had been held and sat through the service. Then we found Harry's grave and put flowers on it, it was so hard to believe Harry was gone, and we missed him so much, but we would never forget him or the happy memories that he had left us with. As time went on it started to get a bit easier. Gradually Gran and Grandad got back to being busy around the farm, and I believe it helped them in a big way to have us to look after. Now spring was coming to an end, and summer was on its way things would get even busier.

We broke up for the summer holidays again, and again there were the gymkhanas and the haymaking. The summer seemed extra busy, which was good because it meant that Gran and Grandad didn't have much time to think about their loss. Brenda saw Joyce every chance she had, they would spend their time discussing their futures, I believe high heel shoes and make up came into the conversation. I would go and play with Jean, as I felt more at home with tea parties and dolls. Mrs Latham said she liked it when I came to play because it gave her a chance to catch up with her work.

The summer holidays went really quickly and

before we knew it we were back at school. It was around this time that Gran came home from town with some news. She said that she had been to the hospital in Nantwich to visit Betty because she had just given birth to Harry's baby girl, no one said much, but I think we were all thinking the same thing, what a wonderful father Harry would have made and how proud he would have been, if only he had lived to see his little girl.

The winter once again set in and soon Christmas was upon us. Not quite the same as other years, Harry wasn't there, and although Gran and Grandad did their best there was a sadness that wouldn't go away. Again we had deep snow that lasted all winter, and would spend our evenings sat by the fire. Spring arrived and so did our birthdays; both Brenda and I were born in April, our birthdays just a few days apart and this was the third birthday that we had spent on the farm, Brenda was now fourteen and I was ten. Although we never had a party, Gran would give us a present and bake a cake to make it a special day.

7

"Good News"

It was during school one morning that one of the teachers came into our classroom, and announced that the war had come to an end. Everyone in the school was dancing around and hugging each other, including Brenda and I, we had all thought that the war would never end, it had lasted for five years and had become a way of life for most people. But my happiness was short lived, "I expect you will be going home soon" a voice said from behind me, I turned to see my teacher smiling at me, " you and Brenda will be able to return to Guernsey, it probably wont be straight away but you must be so excited" she said putting her hand on my shoulder as if to congratulate me. I felt confused, numb but not excited, I had all of a sudden become so mixed up, I had many times in the past prayed that the war would end so that I could go home, when I was alone playing with my tea set in the garage, when I was taking a hiding for something that I hadn't done, but now I was home, my new home, with my new family that I loved. Brenda was quite excited she talked all the way home from school about seeing our mum again, she remembered her much better than I did, but she had been older than I had when we had left, I didn't even remember what my mum looked like, " I'll miss everyone here of course" she said, "but won't it be great Joan," I didn't answer.

When we reached home, Gran told us that she had already heard the news, putting on a brave face she told us that she was pleased that we would be able to see our mum again but that she would miss us ever so much, but that we still had a couple of weeks together as it would take that long for all of the Germans to leave the island, and for the authorities to arrange our transport home. I could hear in her voice, the hurt she was feeling and wanted to cry and tell her that it was all right, I wasn't going to leave. It wasn't that I didn't want to see my mum, but Gran and Grandad were my parents now and I didn't want to leave them.

The next day Gran gave us a letter, to ask the teacher to give us the money that we had saved in our bank. She said that she would take us to Nantwich so that we could buy some material to have new dresses made to wear to go home in. I must admit this cheered me up slightly, I enjoyed going shopping and we chose some lovely material, it was white with blue forget-me-nots all over it, Gran also used the money to buy us new shoes and a new coat each.

At the weekend Gran took us to a dressmaker to

get measured for our new dresses. The dressmaker was a lady that Gran knew, and she lived just down the road from our farm. We arrived at her house and went in through the front gate; all of a sudden a little white dog came pounding towards us down the path, barking frantically. "Just stand still," said Gran, a woman came to the door and called out to the little dog and he ran inside. The woman invited us in and showed us into the lounge, Gran explained that Brenda and I would like her to make us a dress each, the woman took our measurements and after complimenting us on our choice of material, said that there would be enough to make us two dresses each. The woman told Gran to bring us back in a week for another fitting, Gran thanked her, we said goodbye and went home.

A week later we returned for our fitting, but this time Brenda and I went on our own. We entered the gate at the dressmaker's house and as before the little white dog ran towards us barking frantically. But instead of standing quietly like last time, I got a bit nervous because Gran wasn't there and shouted at him, this made him more agitated and he went to bite my leg, realising just in time I quickly dodged behind Brenda and he bit her leg instead. The woman came running out of her house and looked very worried when she realised the dog had bitten Brenda, but Brenda explained that it was my fault for shouting at him and told the woman that he hadn't bitten her too hard. The woman told the little dog off then led us inside to try on our dresses, they weren't quite finished but already we could tell that we would like them. Once the dresses were all pinned the woman told us that we wouldn't need to try them on any more and that Gran could collect them in a couple of days. As we left, the woman said that we were to tell Gran about her dog biting Brenda, and to say how sorry she was, she then said goodbye and wished us a safe journey home to Guernsey.

A couple of days later when we got home from school Gran had been to collect our dresses, we tried them on for Gran and Grandad to see and they both said that the dresses looked lovely. Brenda and I were both delighted with them and although I wasn't looking forward to going home I was quite looking forward to wearing my new dress with my new shoes and coat. "Take your dresses and put one on a hanger, and pack one in your case" said Gran "you can wear the one on the hanger to travel," she said. She smiled as she spoke, but you could detect sadness in her voice, although she tried hard to hide it.

It was two weeks after the war had ended that when we returned from school, Gran had news about us going home. It was to be next Tuesday morning and Gran said that she would take us at the weekend to visit all the neighbours so that we could say goodbye to everyone. Up until now, although we had been told that we would be going home, we didn't know when, and somehow being told that we were leaving on Tuesday made leaving a reality. When the weekend arrived saying goodbye to everyone was much harder than we could have imagined. First Gran took us to the Stewart's, Mrs Stewart gave us a big hug, and Mr Stewart said in a teasing sort of way that he would miss his little potato pickers. Then we went to Mrs Darlington and thanked her again for the flowers that she had let us pick, she laughed and said that there was no need to thank her and she hoped we would have a good trip home. Next we went to the Latham's, I was sad to say goodbye to them, they had been very special neighbours, and I knew I would miss them, especially Jean. By the time we left the Latham's the tears had started trickling down my face, I tried to wipe them away before anyone noticed but as we neared home, Alf, the Latham's farm hand came over to us. Mrs Latham had told him that we were leaving and he had chased after us to say goodbye. "I'm sorry to hear you are leaving, who am I going to tease now?" he said giving us a big smile. I liked Alf he was always happy, and by this time I couldn't hide my tears any more and instead of trickling they were pouring down my face, much faster than I could wipe them away. These were all my friends and I didn't know if I would ever see them again, I would miss them all so much. Gran said that she thought we should go home now and visit the Hedges on Sunday as I was far too upset to go today. We went home and spent the rest of the day wondering around the farm as if visiting each place or animal not knowing if we would have time to visit them again. It was a really strange feeling, it was almost as though it was all a bad dream and I would eventually wake up.

The following day Gran took us up to say goodbye

to Mr and Mrs Hedge, they said that they were sorry that we were leaving, but were pleased to hear that we would be seeing our mum again. Brenda was quite upset at having to leave Joyce; they had become very close friends, and would never forget each other.

Monday morning was our last day at school and at the end of the day before we left, the teachers and all the children wished us well and said that they would miss us. We had been the only evacuees at our school and everyone had treated us a bit special. We had liked our school, and because it was so small we knew everyone that went there.

When we got home Gran had been sorting out our clothes, she had packed them neatly in our cases all accept the clothes we would wear to travel. We wandered up to the barn where Grandad was milking the cows. Brenda and I took turns in holding the cows tails for the last time, then when Grandad had finished we patted all of the cows one by one to say goodbye. We wandered around the farm as if leaving were all a dream or in my case a nightmare. We spent a while with Jack, he was all grown up now, but we still thought of him as our pet. He was gentle and still sucked our hands if we let him. Gran called us in for tea, it was strange, we all sat at the table eating as if it was a normal day, but it was far from normal, it was our last day and tomorrow we would be leaving. After tea Gran said we were best to have our baths and have an early night as we had a long day travelling ahead of us. We had our bath and got ready for bed.

All I could think of was how I was going to tell everyone that I wasn't leaving, that I was happy here and loved Gran and Grandad but I couldn't leave Brenda either so she would have to stay as well.

I didn't sleep much that night, five years had passed since we had left Guernsey and our mum. I didn't really remember her and I was sure she wouldn't remember us either, after all I was ten now, and Brenda fourteen, we were grown up and nothing like we were five years ago when we left. I was sure that once we explained to our mum that we were happy here she would understand, perhaps even come and visit us. I eventually went to sleep, planning how I would explain to everyone in the morning that it would be best if we stayed here, and perhaps our mum could visit so that we could see her again.

Early the next morning Gran called us down to breakfast. Brenda and I both got dressed in the clothes that had been laid out for us to travel in; we had our new dresses that had been especially made for us, and our new shoes and socks. It was quite nice putting them on, but I felt as though there wasn't much point as I didn't intend going anywhere. "Brenda" I said in a determined voice " I don't think we should go, after all Gran and Grandad need us here to help them on the farm" Brenda just looked at me as if I were mad " what are you talking about" she said, "we're going home to see our mum, aren't you excited" I didn't know what to say, how could I tell her that I didn't remember my mum, that I wanted to stay here. "Yes I would like to see her" I said "but I think Gran and Grandad need us more, after all they have not long lost Harry and have no one to look after them". "Don't be silly Joan they'll be fine, come on get your bag". Brenda picked up her suitcase and her gas mask and went downstairs.

I picked up my case and gas mask and followed her downstairs. It would be alright I thought, Gran and Grandad love us they won't let us go. Gran had made a big breakfast for us, and her and Grandad sat at the table to eat with us for the last time. After breakfast Gran told us to put on our coats as we would have to leave to get to the school in time to catch the bus. Grandad gave us both a big hug and a kiss on the cheek, " I will miss you both very much" he said, "it has been so nice to have you both living with us" and with tears in his eyes he smiled at us and said "Perhaps one day you will come back and see us." Gran gave us an extra bag to take with us, she said that she had heard Guernsey people had been short of things during the war, and had put a few bits and pieces in the bag for our mum. It was time to leave; Grandad gave us one last hug as Gran led us out of the door. We had to walk to school quite quickly as there was a bus picking up evacuees from all the different schools and it was due to pick us up from the school quite soon.

I walked in a trance not quite understanding what was happening, I was sure that Grandad wouldn't let us go, that he would say that he wanted us to stay, but here we were going for the bus and he had said goodbye. I didn't understand, I was sure he loved us, yet he had let us go.

We reached the school at the same time as the bus that had come to collect us. Gran grabbed hold of us both hugging us as tight as she could She started sobbing and saying that she loved us. Brenda and I were both crying and hugging her back. " I don't want to go" I cried "please Brenda can't we stay here". A woman got off of the bus and held Brenda's hand and mine, "come on girls" she said "Its time to go home". Gran let go of us and tried to dry her eyes, "Now you come back and see me one day," she said trying to talk as if she were alright, but you could hear in her voice that her heart was breaking. The woman led us onto the bus, and although I wanted with all my heart to pull away from her and run back to Gran. I knew deep down in my heart that it wouldn't do any good. It didn't make any difference what Gran or Grandad wanted, or even what Brenda or I wanted, we belonged with our mum and she wanted us back.

The door of the bus closed behind us and we sat next to each other on the seat both still crying we looked out of the window to see Gran stood with her hand over her mouth and tears streaming down her face. As the bus drove off Gran was waving goodbye her face disfigured with the pain of losing us. It was like a bad nightmare, it felt as though in my whole life I had been taken away from the people I loved, and the people that loved me, why couldn't things have just stayed as they were, we were all happy, and surely our mum would have understood, after all she had lived five years without us.

It must have been so hard for Gran, for over two years she had cared for us as though we were her own, and on top of that she had lost Harry. As the bus drove off Brenda and I just sat crying, Brenda wanted to go home, but loved Gran and Grandad as much as I did and had found it hard to leave, at least she remembered our mum, as hard as I tried I couldn't even remember what she looked like.

8

"Going Home"

The bus that we were in was full of evacuees returning home, some excited at seeing their families again and some like me, devastated at being taken away from the family they had become to think of as their own. We were only on the bus a short while, I sat huddled on the seat next to Brenda, tears streaming down my face, all I could think of was Gran and Grandad and how I wanted to go home to them.

The bus pulled in at a railway station and we were all taken off of the bus and led through the station to the platform to wait for trains that had been put on especially to take us to Southampton. We were quite surprised when we saw how many other children were already waiting for the train, all carrying their gas masks and bags and wearing name tags, just like us. The people who were there to look after us told us to sit on our cases quietly as we had a long wait for the train. Brenda and I found a space and sat down. Gran had packed some sandwiches and a drink to have on our journey. We decided we were already getting hungry so now was a good time to eat as any, so we tucked in. All the time we were sat there more children were arriving, the station was packed.

Eventually the train arrived and the children started to pile on, Brenda and I quickly found two seats together as the seats were filling fast. There were children everywhere. As soon as our train was full it pulled away from the station, and as it picked up speed some of the children on board started to sing. Before long all of the children were joining in, including us. We sang songs like 'It's a long way to Tipperary' and 'Pack up your troubles in your old kit bag,' we even sang 'Sarnia Cherie,' Guernseys anthem, Although I had never heard it before. It must have been quite a heart moving experience for the people minding us to hear hundreds of children singing a song about the island they had left five years before, a song that describes a longing to return to that island. Unfortunately it didn't describe how I felt, and although I was singing with the others I still wanted to go back to Gran, and wondered if she was alright.

We were a long time on the train and by the time we arrived in Southampton we were very tired and hungry and wished we hadn't eaten our sandwiches so early. Everyone was transferred straight from the train onto busses that took us to the boat. I was so tired that I fell asleep on the bus. By the time we arrived at the boat it was dusk, it took quite a while to get all of the children on board, but eventually the boat was loaded and we were on the last stage of our journey.

We were given a hot drink and a sandwich, and then shown to where we were to spend the night. Brenda and I had bunk beds, Brenda had the bottom one and I slept on the top. Not long after we were in bed someone came to check that we were alright and asked if we would like anything else to eat or drink, but although we were still hungry we were too tired to eat and said we just wanted to go to sleep. Within minutes I was sound, but after sleeping a while I woke up feeling really sick. I quickly jumped out of bed forgetting that I was on the top bunk and went sprawling across the floor. Everyone woke up when they heard the thud, and a couple of ladies ran over to see if I was alright, but it was only my pride that was hurt. I explained to one of the ladies that I felt sick and she fetched me a bag and a drink of water then sat with me for a while. Eventually I returned to bed and managed to get back to sleep.

In the morning we were woken up early and told to make sure that we had all of our things. We were given instructions on how to get off of the boat safely, we had to leave in pairs and walk carefully down the gangplank without running. The boat docked in Guernsey and we all did as we had been told, everyone left the boat and were once again put unto busses. We were driven to the end of the white rock harbour where the busses parked in a row, people were boarding the busses looking for their children and one by one the children were being found by their parents and taken home. Our bus was nearly empty and Brenda and I were still sat in the back waiting because no one had yet come to claim us. "Go and ask the driver if he knows where our mum is" said Brenda. I made my way to the front of the bus and tapped the driver on the shoulder, he looked around "our mum hasn't collected us" I said. A lady that was stood in the doorway asked "are you Joan Patch?" I turned to look at her "Yes" I said "are you my mum," The ladies eyes filled with tears as she said "yes Joan I am," I shouted out to the back of the bus, "Brenda I've found her," Brenda collected her stuff and joined me, we both got off the bus, our mum grabbed us both and hugged us so tight that I could hardly breath. Brenda was hugging her back and crying, and I realised that this was the moment that Brenda had been longing for, for five years. As for me, I was once again very confused. I hadn't recognised my mum but it was obvious that Brenda had.

It was after mum had finished hugging us, we realised that there were other people there to meet us. Our mum introduced us to them, one after the other; they were all members of our family that I had long forgotten, our Grandad and our uncle Stan (he was the one that had put the chicken in my Christmas sack) and our auntie Flo. Uncle Stan picked up our cases, we gave the bag of goodies to our mum that Gran had given us for her and we all started walking to what was to be our new home.

Our mum had moved while we had been away and our new home was a flat in town so we didn't have far to walk. Our Grandad, uncle and aunt came in and had a cup of tea and a piece of cake before they went home. My mum had said that she hoped that we would like living here and not miss living on a farm too much, uncle Stan had suggested that she bought a cow and kept it in the back yard to make us feel more at home, we all laughed and that broke the ice a bit as we were all feeling very awkward, but after they left I started feeling a bit uncomfortable and very homesick.

There had been a great shortage of food in the island during the war and still was. What little food there was was on ration. I remember we queued for nearly an hour just to be able to buy some ham. The Red Cross used to send in food parcels which were a great help, and Brenda and I would take turns in opening them, it was good fun looking to see what they had sent.

It took a while but eventually we settled into our new life. Our mum used to work to keep us, as there was no help available for one-parent families in those days. She worked for a really nice family doing their housework. It wasn't long before I realised why Brenda had wanted to come home to our mum so much. She would do anything for us, and worked hard to keep us, and although I still missed Gran and Grandad I now felt I probably had the best mum in the world, and was starting to love her very much.

It was a year after we had returned to Guernsey that the family that my mum worked for paid for all three of us to go to Cheshire to visit Gran and Grandad. Brenda and I were both really excited at the thought of seeing them again, we could only stay a couple of days, but at least we could see if they were all right, and our mum could thank them in person for looking after us so well.

Our return to Cheshire was a great surprise for Gran and Grandad, and they were ever so pleased to see us again and to meet our mum. It was good to see that they were both alright and the farm hadn't changed at all. We saw the Latham's, and Brenda got a chance to visit Joyce, but all too soon it was time to leave. It had been nice to see them all again and I still loved Gran and Grandad dearly, but when it was time to go I didn't mind, I was going home with my mum, and knew that Gran and Grandad were fine.

Over the next few months we wrote a few times, but Gran was not one for letter writing and eventually we lost contact. Our lives were normal at last. I liked my school and had made new friends. Brenda had started work and we were happy living with our mum in our flat, which we now thought of as home.

Joan and Brenda 1946 - Back at home, one year after the war ended.

9

"Years Later"

The years went by, Brenda and I both married. Brenda had seven children, and I had five. In 1974 we lost our mum, it was devastating, she had looked out for us all of our lives and always put us first, but our children now depended on us, as we had on her, and this somehow helped us through, and as before Brenda and I still had each other.

It was exactly fifty years after the war that Brenda's family gave her a surprise birthday present. Two return tickets to Cheshire so that we could both go back to see the place where we had lived.

It was truly amazing, we thought that all of the people that we had known would either have died or moved away. We knew that Gran and Grandad would no longer be alive, as they were quite old when we lived with them.

We arrived in Cheshire and booked into a small inn in Nantwich for our week's holiday. That evening we went for a walk around the town, then the following morning we found a taxi and asked the driver to take us to Ridley square, which was the junction at the end of the road from the Jackson's farm. The taxi driver dropped us off reluctantly, asking if we were sure we would be alright as we were in the middle of nowhere. We assured him that we would be fine, so after warning us that the traffic was horrific, and telling us to call him if we needed a lift back, the taxi driver drove off, leaving us at the side of the road.

Well he was right about the traffic, it was scary, there was huge lorries of all descriptions, passing us at an unbelievable speed. It was nothing like that peaceful road that we had walked along so many times all those years ago. When the only time we seemed to see any traffic was when the American convoys had passed, and the soldiers had thrown us sweets. We started making our way down the road towards the farm we had once known as home, keeping well in by the hedge. We passed the Darlington's house and wondered if any of the family still lived there, but didn't stop. We just kept walking until we reached the Latham's farm. We walked across the yard to the front door remembering all the times we had been here to deliver the papers. It felt like it was only a couple of weeks ago, the memory was so clear, not fifty years. We knocked on the door and a young man answered, "Hello" he said with a look of surprise on his face, "what can I do for you".

Brenda explained that we were trying to trace some people who we had known during the war, a Mr and Mrs Latham. The man looked quite amazed, "that was my Gran and Grandad," he said. "They died some time ago, their son John and his wife ran the farm until they retired, and built a house just along the road" the man explained "I am sure John and his wife would love to meet you," We thanked him and said that we would go and visit John.

It was just a little way along the road that we found John's house, we guessed it must be the right one, as it was the only new house that had been built since we had left all those years ago. We knocked at the door but there was no answer, and it was starting to rain so we decided to leave, just as we started walking down the path a car pulled into the drive. A man and a woman got out, they both looked quite surprised to see two women at their house. "Hello, can we help you?" the man asked. Brenda and I looked at each other and smiled. Brenda turned to him and said, "You're John Latham aren't you?" "Yes", the man replied with a puzzled look on his face. "I don't suppose you remember us?" Brenda asked. The man studied us both, but looked even more puzzled than before, and by now his wife was getting curious. "We lived here during the war years at Mr and Mrs Jackson's farm" I said, feeling it was time to put them out of their misery. The woman walked over to us and introduced herself, " I'm Muriel" she said, "Come on inside and have a cup of tea and a chat."It was a beautiful house, and they made us feel very welcome. They showed us into the sitting room where Muriel served us tea and biscuits. "Now tell us all about yourselves", she said. John just sat speechless, but still looked puzzled, as if he was finding it hard to remember us. We explained how we had been evacuated during the war and that we lived on the farm down the road with an elderly couple called Mr and Mrs Jackson whom we called Gran and Grandad and that they'd had a son, called Harry, who had died while we were living there. Muriel asked how long we had lived at the farm, "nearly three years" I replied. We said how we knew Mr and Mrs Latham and their children Marshal, John and Jean, although Jean had only been three years old, I told Muriel how I used to go to the Latham's farm and play with Jean after school. Muriel looked intrigued although John still looked a bit vague.

There were so many questions that we wanted to ask them. John told us that Gran and Grandad had died quite a few years ago, and that another elderly couple now lived at the farm. Sadly we learned that Jean had died when she was quite young. We asked about Mr and Mrs Hedge and their daughter Joyce, John explained that Joyce lived somewhere near Nantwich, and was married with a family, her mother and father were both dead, and there was no longer a house up in the fields where they had lived. "I don't suppose you remember a farm hand that worked on your farm, he was called Alf, he used to tease me, and call me his little scallywag", I asked John, not really expecting him to know who I was talking about. John and Muriel looked at each other in amazement. Muriel reached for the phone, "I just need to make a call," she said, with no further explanation. She dialled a number and after a few seconds said, "Hello Alf, how are you", after hearing his answer she said "I just phoned to ask you, if you remember two evacuee girls that lived on the Jackson's farm", Muriel held the receiver out so that Brenda and I could hear Alf's reply. " Yes of course I do, Brenda and Joan" he said, "Well they are sat here having a cup of tea with John and me". Alf went quiet then after a few minutes he said, "They're not are they?" Brenda and I both laughed at his reaction. Muriel promised Alf, that she would take us to visit him before we returned to Guernsey. We thanked Muriel and John, but said that we would have to go as we wanted to see the farm that had been our home before we went back to Nantwich. Muriel insisted that when we had seen the farm we return to her house so that she could give us a lift back to our hotel.

Brenda and I left and walked further down the road to the farm where we had lived. We were so sad to think that Gran and Grandad were no longer there as we neared the farm we could see the barns and stables, but they were all closed up as it was no longer used as a farm. The elderly man who lived there was working in the garden and when he saw us looking he came over and said hello. We told him why we were there and how we had lived in his house fifty years ago. "You must come in and meet my wife," he said, so we followed him into the house. It was really strange, the living room had been made into a bedroom and the kitchen was now a kitchen-diner. They were a nice couple and they made us very welcome, but all the time we were there we just felt sad to think that Gran and Grandad were no longer there, and that the farm was no longer a farm. The place that Brenda and I had spent three happy years had lost its magic.

We thanked the couple for inviting us into their home, and then we went back to John and Muriel who gave us a lift back to Nantwich. When we got out of the car Muriel told us that she would pick us up the next day, and take us for a drive.

Once back at our inn we phoned the taxi driver to let him know that we had got back safely, as he was expecting us to call him when we wanted to return. He was quite surprised to learn that after all these years we had managed to find people that we knew, and thanked us for phoning.

The next morning as promised Muriel came to the inn to collect us, she told us that she had managed to contact Joyce Hedge, and had taken it upon herself to arrange a meeting for us with her the next day. Brenda was delighted, and turning to me said, "fancy seeing Joyce again after all those years". Muriel took us in her car to see Alf, when we arrived he was waiting on his doorstep for us to get there. It was so strange to see him; he was quite old and had retired. I remembered him as a young man full of energy. He gave us both a hug, and said, "Come in and meet my wife". He took us in and introduced us to her; they seemed to make the perfect couple. They made us all a cup of tea, and we all had a chat about old times. It was good talking to Alf, he remembered us living there, but was quite surprised at how well we remembered him.

When we left Alf's house, Muriel took us to see Mr and Mrs Stewart's daughter, her mum and dad had died quite a few years ago but she remembered us very well, and like everyone else was amazed and pleased to see us.

Next Muriel asked if we would like to see our old school, we said that we would love to, so she drove us back along the road that we had walked so many times, it was a strange feeling, it almost felt like we had never left, we remembered how we used to shout out to the American convoys, "got any gum chum" and how we would quickly eat our sweets, so that Gran wouldn't get cross with us, it was like stepping back in time. We arrived at the school, it was now used as a place for boxing food, and there were people working there. We went inside, Muriel knew the people who were in charge and explained to them why we were there. They were only too happy to show us around; when we came out I looked at the place where the bus had stopped to take us back to Guernsey. I could picture Gran and could have cried, thinking how upset she had been.

At the end of the day Muriel took us back to Nantwich, on the way there she showed us where Joyce was going to meet us the next afternoon, and said that she would phone us before we went back to Guernsey.

The next morning after breakfast we went for a walk around the town and bought some presents to take home for our families. We saw the open market where we had sold our mushrooms and I had bought my bracelet. Then we bought some flowers and went to see if we could find Gran and Grandad's grave, but sadly we couldn't find theirs or Harry's. We found out from the local registry office which cemetery they were buried in, but couldn't find their names on any of the head stones. So we just put the flowers on one of the unmarked graves.

After lunch we set out to meet Joyce. When we arrived at the place, Muriel had pointed out to us, sure enough there was a lady waiting there. We walked over to her, and Brenda said, "You must be Joyce," "yes" said Joyce and gave us both a hug. She had her car with her, and asked us if we would like to go for a drive. She took us way out in the country, where we stopped and had tea at a very picturesque teashop, that had five or six little gift shops surrounding it. Brenda and Joyce had so much to talk about, telling each other all that had happened since the war. I was pleased to see Joyce, but it was so good to see Brenda enjoying herself with her old friend, so I sat back and let them do most of the talking. The afternoon passed quickly, and in no time at all we were back in Nantwich, saying goodbye to Joyce.

We only had one full day left and kept that day to stroll around Nantwich buying our last few presents to take home. In the morning Muriel had phoned us, she asked if her and John could take us out for an evening meal, and we said that would be very nice. So when we got back from shopping we packed our bags ready to leave the next morning. That evening Muriel and John picked us up and took us to a hotel, just outside of Nantwich. We had a lovely meal, and they would not let us pay for anything. It was a perfect end to a perfect holiday. We had met so many people from our past, and it was mostly because of Muriel. She had been so helpful, and was a lovely person whom strangely enough was the one person we had not known before.

That last night we went to bed and reflected on what had happened. Somehow it had seemed quite magical, and far outweighed our expectations.

I am seventy years old now, retired, with time on my hands, and thought it would be nice to write what it was like for me as an evacuee. People come and go, but memories last forever, and although we could never love anyone as much as our mum, Cheshire and its people will always hold a special place in our hearts.

Brenda and Joyce Hedge (1995) on our return visit, fifty years after the war ended.